CREATURE

Also by Michael Dumanis

My Soviet Union

CREATURE

Michael Dumanis

Four Way Books
Tribeca

for my mother

Library of Congress Cataloging-in-Publication Data

Names: Dumanis, Michael, 1976- author.
Title: Creature / Michael Dumanis.
Identifiers: LCCN 2023004560 (print) | LCCN 2023004561 (ebook) | ISBN 9781954245761 (trade paperback) | ISBN 9781954245778 (ebook)
Subjects: LCGFT: Poetry.
Classification: LCC PS3604.U46 C74 2023 (print) | LCC PS3604.U46 (ebook) | DDC 811/.6--dc23/eng/20230206
LC record available at https://lccn.loc.gov/2023004560
LC ebook record available at https://lccn.loc.gov/2023004561

2nd printing, 2024
This book is manufactured in the United States of America and printed on acid-free paper.

Four Way Books is a not-for-profit literary press. We are grateful for the assistance we receive from individual donors, public arts agencies, and private foundations including the New York State Council on the Arts, a state agency.

We are a proud member of the Community of Literary Magazines and Presses.

Contents

Notes

He weeps by the side of the ocean,

  He weeps on the top of the hill;

He purchases pancakes and lotion,

  And chocolate shrimps from the mill.

—Edward Lear
  "How Pleasant to Know Mr. Lear"

Natural History

I'm fully posable, a leather and clay creature
with the capacity to waltz and do the Twist.
My jaws unclench themselves. My eyes swing open.
The world is young, and I still have some years,
so I take out a patent on slow-moving fog.
Take out a patent on the hyacinth.
I brand the cow. Trademark the coelacanth:
its tiny heart is shaped like a straight tube.
However, the darkness keeps hitting
me over the head with its hammer.
I want to feel more substantial
than an elephant wearing a fez,
so I invent the Theory of Gravity,
so I discover my larynx and use it,
so I study yoga and learn how to wrap
my legs around my neck, but I keep finding
occasion to lie on the floor like a slug
or weep into the rented furniture,
so I invent the Bhagavad Gita,
so I invent the Gutenberg Bible,
so I invent the Etch-a-Sketch and draw
myself a lover with the right proportions,
we go on holiday and sit in traffic,
I do my best not to erase her, not to shake

things up. When we get lonely, we invent

the baby, a fully posable

leather and clay creature. It cries

like a small bird. We pose with it.

To never erase you, I carve your initials,

my lover, into the spine of a tree. You are happy

but the tree dies. So I take out a patent

on the synthetic tree, and I carve

your initials, my lover, into its torso,

and take you to the disco and the roller derby,

to the waterfall beside the paper mill.

It's so amazing what we get to see.

The ruins extend across the valleys, toward each sea.

Autobiography

Attempted avoiding abysses, assorted
abrasions and apertures, abscesses.

At adolescence, acted absurd: acid,
amphetamines. Amorously aching

after an arguably arbitrary Abigail,
authored an awful aubade.

Am always arabesquing after Abigails.
Am always afraid: an affliction?

Animals augur an avalanche. Animals
apprehend abattoirs. Am, as an animal,

anxious. Appendages always aflutter,
am an amazing accident: alive.

Attired as an apprentice aerialist,
addressed acrophobic audiences.

Aspiring, as an adult, after applause,
attracted an angelic acolyte.

After an affirming affair, an abortion.
After an asinine affair, Avowed Agnostic

approached, alone, an abbey's altarpiece,
asking Alleged Almighty about afterlife.

Ambled, adagio, around an arena.
Admired an ancient aqueduct. Ate aspic.

Adored and ate assorted animals.
Ascended an alp. Affected an accent.

Acquired an accountant, an abacus, assets.
Attempted atonal arpeggios.

Skull of a Unicorn

Sculptures are ghosts.
Your head is an object.

You are an object
in the question, *What happened to you?*

The animals, just-born,
are uniformly moist, benign.

Bandaged
in glistening skin.

Grown larger, they begin
to hunt each other.

There's more beyond / but not too much.
This is a study / for a massacre.

We are like everyone unique
infused with the spirit of pain.

And you, one sorry horse's
severed head some joker fixed

a spire of scintillating crystal to:

what happened to you?

The Courtship

One kisses one with one's skull face.
One holds one in one's bone embrace.
One holds one in one's dress's folds.
One folds one into one's dress's folds.

One takes one in. One has been taken in.
One runs for blocks after the ice cream truck.
One triumphs in a war. "We won,"
one warns the other, vanquished one.

One writes the poem, "Melancholia in Passaic."
One writes the poem, "Late Frost in Bergen County."
Walking the length of the Great Wall of China,
one passes one one loves. One doesn't turn.

One's body has become a living sculpture
displayed to the public until the limit
of extreme exhaustion. One is extremely exhausted.
One gives away one's furniture and pens.

For years, one holds one in the flickering brain.
The other tries to pass one, but one turns.
Two spend one afternoon watching the bees
fit their soft bodies into the blue flowers.

Each day each thinks, *did we unplug the iron?*
Each day each thinks, *we help God make the stars.*
Until the limit of extreme exhaustion,
singing, each body slashes at the white fog.

Our replacements arrive. They look
awfully like us. We keep being the last
to leave the beach. It is always the others
who die. There is no solution

because there is no problem.
The trees grow out of one another slowly,
the thief who breaks into the car takes nothing,
and everything, until it's not, is fine.

State of the Union

We paint the bedroom walls Quixotic Plum.
We paint the bedroom ceiling Foggy Day.

You paint your nails and eyelids Peacock Blue.
We drive to photograph the flying buttresses

of the flamboyant oil refinery
and stay through dusk to catch the glimmering

reflections of its lights against the Ship Channel,
and also the striated moon in the water,

rippling alongside, an incontrovertible fact.
You whisper, *How much would it cost*

to reupholster the Chrysler? You are as elegant
as a grand piano. You throw tantrums

for a living. You make a good living.
Everyone is rich, for a little while.

Everyone is happy, for a little while,
even a day is a very long time,

and for a while the spoons and butter knives
continue to reflect our sunburnt masks.

For years we act astonishingly lifelike,
running one's lips across the other's thorax,

painting the stairs and hallways Golden Fleece.
It would be nice to believe in a God.

Children step out of our curtains
and ask us to hold them.

Ours is the only of possible worlds:
femur, pubis, ribcage, sternum, clavicle.

We close our eyes when we get tired
of looking at each other. In my dream,

it is always the same: having painted
my breath Frost and my hair Quicksilver,

I stand with my luggage outside, getting ready
to board the slow train to Albania;

the night is heavy but her skin is soft.
Night comes at me across the lawn until I fall.

She covers my mouth with her novocaine mouth.
Little torpedoes of grass shard my back.

Night paws at me with her five thousand hands,
then rubber-bands her limbs around my neck.

She prays into my ears. They turn to moss.
Possibly, this is the only end: dust,

the star-addled, wind-saddled black
flag of the sky waving over us.

When I grow up, I do not want to be a headstone.
When I grow up, I want to be a book.

Squalor

In the beginning, I thought a great deal
about death and sunlight, et cetera,
cramming each syllable that I could cram
into the seconds and brackets allotted me,
all for the memoir that wouldn't be written,
all for the movie that wouldn't be made.
Look at the way I ran after you, arms
stirring dust as you wondered out loud,
glancing up at the skylights, if they needed cleaning.
The walls shed their plaster. Our credit is bad,
and the collection agency has sent its men.
We've had a hard time. We're becoming
a little bit scared. The sudden daughter
shivers through the room. We used to be shiny
and flexible robots. That wasn't a wound
in my back, not a knife, but a key.
The sudden daughter tells us the bad dream:
I tried to kiss him but he had no mouth.
What will be left of her in eighty years.
In the television version of the trials of my life,
the one on all night in a room in my skull,
canned laughter punctuates each time I speak,
the background music swells when I enter.
Does it relieve me or scare me

that I might have made an impression.
If I had a choice, would I rather
tend to a yard or an ocean.
Sometimes one stands in the Price Chopper
parking lot, waiting for the Rapture.
In Cleveland, I can only get a pierogi
as a topping on my hot dog
when the pierogi chef comes in
but I can always order a pierogi stuffed
inside a sauerkraut and grilled cheese sandwich.
We take a vacation. We get vulnerably drunk.
From time to time, the usual moment
seems endless.

Greater Bilby

This article only concerns itself
with greater bilbies, the extant
species of bilby. For the extinct
species of bilby, see
lesser bilby. How many people
have seen a bilby
or know what a bilby is?
Unlike other bandicoots, I
make an excellent burrower.
This blue-grey fur with patches
of tan feels soft like a receding
childhood in the dimming thought
of a lonely traveler. My sense of smell
is better than yours as I hurtle
along the barrens like a tiny
rocking horse. My fluted hairless
ears are the slenderest oyster shells.
I, like you, harbor unrequited
romantic feelings for God,
prefer the comfort of a nightfall
to the hot glare of anything.
Perhaps we must develop
a new appreciation. Fewer greater
bilbies than pygmy elephants soak up

the fraying, fragrant atmosphere,
than Ganges river dolphins. Once
bilbies skittered through Adelaide
gleefully. Pin the whatever
on the whatever. The pages
of this encyclopedia I clamor through
wear thin. Soon I may see
in the dust my little cousin again.
For the time being, I presume
a future, and scratching for a termite
the hard soil around the bunchgrass,
unhinge my small jaw, proffer
my endless tongue.

The Double Dream of Spring

The last giraffe, the final chanterelle,
you in the window of the double dream of spring,

the lifting drawbridge, the remaining breath
lifting the drawbridge to the locked dream.

But for two clouds, the sky retains its color
as the hot air balloon ascends like a soft head.

A boy in a felt pirate hat, I followed
a red ball into the shimmering woods.

The red ball lay in the woods.
The woods gathered around the red ball.

Searching in vain the barbed undergrowth,
idly resolving to turn myself into

a mapmaker or a ventriloquist, poet or god,
O what a ball I had, spending the days.

A man fitted into a frock coat, I feel followed
by the conspiring skyline of mountains.

Tempted as I am, I won't slink off
for now for good into its granite embrace.

Tracing my hand over the stony bones
that, fused together, hold my only face,

sparing some time before the impending extinction,
I stand in the clearing between two pages of forest

and recognize myself.

Checkpoint

I crossed a border, I crossed a line, I crossed a threshold, I crossed a divide,
I forded the strait between nowhere and wish, I shifted my body's weight
in the direction of the sun, I was born in a well and began to crawl up
toward a light in the muck, I believed I'd be well
were I anywhere else, so I threw myself up
but nobody caught me as I dropped down, so I threw myself up
every day for a life, the stone earth below me my hard trampoline,
a hiss in the throat telling me what I needed, to live
in a bleached neighborhood in the shade of high trees
that bounced their helicopter fruit against the breeze,
so I believed a promise on the side of the imagined line I wasn't on,
like softer bread or bolder shade of sky,
a promise like another me with a changed name and posture, were I
to cross the border, to cross the line, to cross the threshold, to cross the divide
seared into the map in my head, so I spent my last coins
on papers and gear, leaving my mother asleep in her chair
as I rushed open-armed toward the door made of air
that the gathering dust storm began to blow shut,
my faith in nothing other than each breath,
also invisible.

The Kidnapped Children

Some of us remember our parents
as shadows capable of song
who smelled of salt each time they leaned toward us
their foggy branches. We were well along
on the ill-defined journey, following their kind
yet strident cadences. We had become accustomed
to the mouthful of names they prepared in the dark,
luminous flower, creased feather, my hoped-for one.
Who was it then that dragged us over stones?
Now the rats are in charge, a pageant of gnaw.
They flounce across the avenue, rally the square,
stand upright on hind legs to gauge the crowd.
The rats are winning. Their shadows swoon
over the parking lot of the abandoned mall.

First we were taken by surprise, away, for granted,
but later taken care of, taken in.
A bath was run. We were prohibited from drowning.
A nurse made rounds to clip our fingernails.
Some of us remember only now and then
the prickly scarf our neck slipped through
one nightfall of wind, and the soft eyes
like stars we fail to place, stars we can't locate
in a face that must have held them. Some of us

have no idea who we are, whose neck

we cradled as we piggybacked, and we know better

than to ask help of the wind that propels us, the sunlight

dissolving the snow. Who anyone is

no one knows anymore. At least we have one another.

The Forecast

I carry myself out into the rainswept blur.
I lift my pleasant voice over the coming flood.
I have nothing to do that I'm going to do.
I keep meaning to purchase a dog. I keep waiting

to email you back. When I see you again will
I know who you are? Once I wove you a mask
of rattan and hair. Once I carved you a mask
of painted wood. I brushed my wooden leg

against your wooden leg. We had learned to imitate
each other's breath. When I see you again will
you know who I am? Will you place your words back
into my open mouth? Once I held you for years

in the stones of my eyes. You were an ineluctable act of God.
Into the drainage ditch we hurled our toys.

Audit

We wore white hats and tights, colorful buttons
preventing the wind from undoing our clothes.
Somebody blew into a wooden tube. Another slapped
taut calfskin at regular intervals. The resulting tune
evoked a transgressive experience in the body. The routine
exhalations intensified, became exaltation. The graveyard
shift at the sawdust factory no longer seemed
like the dead end it was. Here we go, we exclaimed to ourselves,
watch us go. Fish-counting by the dry creek bed (largemouth bass
conspicuously absent, no common shiner, no fallfish) was one
of our innumerable pastimes. All we needed
was bossa nova in a darkened room. All we needed
were a bassinet and a basset hound. All we needed we wrote
on our unwashed palms and in the locked shorthand of ledgers.
What is the soul's cryptocurrency? The overpowering sounds
of the respective animals inside us kept us from sleep more frequently
than the medical journals advised. Bottlecap eyes, horned tongue,
we did not like what we gleaned from the mirrors, and the older we turned
the more we remembered. We had been looking forward
to the party, but then we saw the invite list, remembered
a discarded tenderness in the wilderness, took stock of our economic
and romantic relationships with every fellow being. Smashed,
crumpled world. And yet the sunlight has continued to tousle gently
the mussed tops of the trees. We had been so many times told to keep

our eye on the ball, but the ball seems to be missing. Good luck
finding anyone to replace someone: we searched the dunes and the inebriated
light of culinary hotspots, the curvaceous back alleys
of upmarket warehouse districts, an ocean of keys, red yarn
constellations, the chiseled silhouettes of faces left behind
in the mind's mushrooming repository, and no dice,
because we did not understand the game, because we could not follow
its simple rules. The music caused us to resort
to dancing, so we jumped about, then soared
into the chartless galaxies in front of us
like whining birds from a faraway star
hurtling our warbling, pulsating masses
toward blurred apocalypse of soot and creosote.
We have seen the white pavilions in the open field.
Everything will be taken away before it's handed back.

Clouds

Because I was afraid of death
I hid my body in a cloud
of vetiver and citron notes
and thought I could persist forever
as something burdening the air
of any room I had to leave.
I carved my name into a tree,
forgetting that the tree would fall.
Crossing the canvas as my paint peeled off me,
I hollered music out of my small teeth.
I thought I would outlast the weather.
Here is one room I had to leave.
Those are my diamond dust shoes in the corner.
I am a dark shape on a video monitor.

American Enterprise

I built this A-frame in Beacon
I thought you might like
I put out all the stops
An eighteen-hole overture

Miniature balloons
Crowd the periphery
Of the mechanical residential gate
With exaggerated spikes

And protruding metal frame
Someone is always backing up
The circular driveway
The future president

Removes his veil
It isn't me for I am foreign-born
Although I have been naturalized
And now hoist a flag fitfully

I don't interchange normally
With people but I do my best
When my number is called
I will proceed to the reception desk

I have had innumerable opportunities
To sample duck *à l'orange*
A wonder what has happened
To the time   There is no telling

Only amnesia taken into evidence
In the underfunded Hall of Science
It's almost time to watch someone
Dissect a cow's eye   For now I bask

Between the weeping cherry
And the common garden peony
In the unseasonable summer
I don't talk about the — or the — or the (shh)

Once my number is called
For the collective good
After I give over my blood
I can leave at any time

The Mileage

The wind fills my ribcage.
Blood enters my wrist.
I pace one heatscarred
courtyard with no purpose,
then, all day, drive
the road into the car.
The tires burn.
The trees do not stop moving.
There isn't much
to do in Terre Haute.
There isn't much
to do in New York City,
the sky a stern face,
the sky a gauze mouth,
and which is more scary,
the possible permanence
of an idea like *gone*
or the possibly permanent
thrum of the ceiling fan,
static inside me?
In the light-engulfed truck stop,
I hide from my death.
My mouth swells with teeth.
I make love to my sandwich.

I pretend I'm the person
each moment has chosen,
that castles appear
by the roadside and only for me.
The child would like to be
when he grows up
a lightning field, an outburst
of hydrangeas, a ghost, a cloud,
some kind of astronaut
or superhero, and a big black dog.
The child into the house
carries dead birds.
In the imagined future I
arrive beside you,
pretend you're the person
I drove through my life for,
dragging your hand
through my fiberglass hair.
The God that's laughing
at us through the fog
sounds like a wounded
screech owl, but more human.
The crows keep giving
birth to smaller crows.

A child keeps rolling
down the same green hill.
The fog cuts the heads
off the buildings.

Nebraska

I could play the accordion
so I was selected for the amateur propaganda team.
It was very cold. I had to stop up the hole in my shoe.
I used the lid of a tin can.

As far as I can tell, there's nothing
trustworthy about my experience of reality.
I stand on one leg. I stand on the other leg.
I rotate my arms clockwise

and call this exercise. In the home movie
I recognize my coat. Taking my turn
with the mechanical bull at Uncle Ron's
Wild West Saloon I hold on for as long as a minute.

So little happens on a given day,
which is why I play the accordion
until I am riddled with someone's applause,
which is why I drive to Arthur County to see

the hay bale church and the world's smallest courthouse.
If I was a blue jay or some kind of robin
I would fly figure-eights over the cottonwoods.
Despite the wind, I would not curse the wind.

The future is a rumor like the past.
The new anxiety supplants the old anxiety.
The continent I stand my ground on drifts,
which is why I have asked you to marry me.

I am solid gold, I say, and I am capable
of loving you until the final asteroid
hides Omaha under an ocean of ash,
but you're unavailable.

They were on their way to the ocean
when they made their minds up to stay here.
The grass was so tall they picked wildflowers
without stepping down from their horses.

We are all so lucky. It is terrifying.
It is a blue-sky day for all the freezingness.
I blink into the chasm of sunlight endlessly.
I forget my life, but then I remember my life.

East Liverpool, Ohio

I have abandoned
plans I had to matter,
my not-conceived-yet
child, his anxious mother,
the lakeview timeshare
with the Tiffany shade.
In the motel room on the bald
face of the mountain,
I wrote in the margins
of the contingency bible,
It moved me that she knew
the names of trees,
but who needs nature
when the power plants
are beautiful? "Catalpa,
catalpa," she said, "common
hackberry, cedar stump,
pile of driftwood, American
bladdernut, dwarf weeping
pussy willow, hard pine,
lacebark pine, pine, soft pine."
My mouth has been stuck
to the roof of my tongue.
I keep forgetting to look up

and be reminded by the moon
that it's the moon I am supposed
to marvel at. The night I paced
the snow-fringed riverbank
watching the cadmium fuming
from the Corinthian smokestacks,
I heard the factory's breath
whisper over the freeway
the way she used to say into my ear,
"I still exist, I still exist, I still exist,"
just one of her immeasurable
failings. She wouldn't listen
when I claimed the country
had been replaced by a new country,
even after the unsigned
postcard in our letterbox
that read, "I have decided
not to commit suicide, don't worry,"
and the second unsigned
postcard, telling us,
"I have decided not to
commit suicide, worry."
After those, no more postcards.

A Lake in Vermont

A lake is a depression.
I bob up and down,
a person who splutters,
a person who coughs

out of my windpipe into the sharp light,
lily pads choking
the velveteen water.
Each consecutive day

I know less what I'm after.
Each consecutive lake
I float longer and farther
as the lungs swell to their capacity

with unsustainable love
for each subarctic bluet damselfly,
every stray sweetflag
spreadwing dragonfly. I may

or may not reach enlightenment.
I have no memoirs, no memory.
The retina reacts to images.
The mountains ring me.

The Fortune

Past the faint latticework
of ghost trees skirmishing
in snowfields mist
has overcome, I drive
myself through postcards
of Vermont, past pyramids
of firewood, vestigial
wells, neat lines of granite
in a plotted square,
each pointed steeple
a foreboding of what's done,
unwelcome paradox
of prophecy. Mistaking
the hunchbacked gods colluding
along the fringes
of the shrouding haze for mountains,
I book a lifetime
at the Weathervane Motel:
will I enjoy my stay,
or will the gunmetal
shade of this low-hanging sky
stick in my eyes when I close them?
Of the two lanes available
on this unwinding drag, I take the one

that leads, each day, me far from me,
then turn around, arriving every time
at the same door. The future
continues to poll in the margin
of terror. The future remains
unimaginable. I imagine it
blistering with bees, strobing
color and clamor, a child
with an orange balloon
hiding his face, a gargantuan
flower. Asked to recollect
my impressions, alongside
any additional comments
about the exhibition overall,
I find it worth remarking on
the light.

The Whereabouts

Is there a home such a place

To encircle the ears to restrain

The meandering children

Keep the sky from one's shoulders

Police off one's skin

Falsetto on the vinyl

Always scratching one song

I adapt to whichever enclosure

Will help me pretend I have won

At this life with its muttering furnace

Bay window of hills

Turning crimson at fall

Lock inside a damp crawlspace

Each foxtrot of thought

While drowsy children

Stumble through the yard

In their flammable wool

While lightning children

Flash across the fields

But once the intimacies go dark

And each room shares a smell

Once the many-legged bugs

Crowd the wavering bulb

Is there still such a spot

Is there a hope such a thought

How small a home

In the context of space

How small the fat Earth

In the ocean of stars

How small is a poet

How narrow each word

The sky fills with words

As the ice sheet gives way

How insignificant woodsmoke

Eternity schemes

The glimmering prospect

Of giving some hope

Kept put the dead priest

When the soldiers drew close

I will orbit each floor

On which I am permitted

To the vinyl's false drone

I will think myself home

As permanent now

As my waving neighbor

Feeling as rich as the loam

Know every lasting thing

Must disappear

A day the wind will win

Over the wall

Endangered like a soap bubble

As handsome as a cockatoo

I grow attached

To the distressed mauve carpet

I live here   breathe this

Wake into each dawn

Keep silvering

In spite of everything

Sun squalling through the blinds

Ministry of Human Capacities

Before I took my place
on the periphery,
I was a revolutionary, I revolved
on my own axis
like the revolving restaurant
at the top of the broadcasting tower
that televised.
The winter sun was in my eyes
as I shuffled along the concrete.
I was a black umbrella slicking
at twilight down Karl Marx Allee.
I could have attained samsara
but I was denounced to the Central Committee.
I went groping and clapping.
I hopped around laughing, a fragrant
drunk, a hermit's soulmate.
Sometimes I felt like a two-headed rooster
but I didn't tell anyone.
I lived in a country that doesn't exist.
I went to Leipzig once, and once
to the North Sea, where I took off my clothes
and kicked at the beach like an egg-laying tortoise,
then entered the cold water lovingly,
my arms and legs becoming magic wands.

It is important to remember what is better
to forget than to remember, what is better
unspoken to the radio in the floor.

Pastoral

I was excited to see every sanctuary,
jaguar, then sloth.
The bright fluted flowers taller than any
in central New Jersey
welcomed me along the periphery
of the dusty byway.
I spotted a kinkajou loping
over a telephone wire as awkwardly
as a three-legged cat
in a Walmart parking lot.
To find out what it was
I had to Google it!
And even the blue jays
so common to me
were an epiphany! Here
in the cloud forest! Surrounded
by fronds and a network of curious
bats angling toward me,
I crossed a rope bridge
over a crevasse as if
in a special exhibit on tropics
in the botanical gardens
of Columbus, Ohio. On the bus
between beaches, a whispering

45

local offered each seat the chance
to buy contraband turtle eggs.
He was taken up
in my memory, eagerly.
There was a great worry constantly
radiating through my arms
and my jawbone, a fire alarm
going inside my chest I couldn't
turn off, smelling the blood
yield to smoke
in my arteries. I was convinced
I needed to find who I was
to make my life give my life
the illusion of purpose. This is why
I left behind everything,
but the holiday destination
with its swaying trees
wouldn't tell me,
so I Googled, *who am I,*
and the predictive text,
presuming I was searching for
the lyrics to a mediocre song,
suggested: *to be loved by you.*
Still, I felt grateful for the sudden

glory of two morpho butterflies
as blue as the deep God-summoning
blue glass of Sainte-Chapelle
in Paris, where I remained a blur
for a good hour once
in hope of finding who I was,
cavorting in a DNA-like
figure-eight before me
as they mated, guilelessly,
through the abundant silver air
during their several
weeks in existence.

Garden of Earthly Delights

Butterflies swarm us.
I never stop talking,

wearing a gown of ivory satin,
my fitted bodice encrusted with seed pearls.

Between the hourglass and the giant harp,
where God is a lemon the beetles infest,

light separates the bodies.
The water surrounding us dances.

In the face of the lagoon,
the cracked teacups.

In the face of the lagoon,
the intersection of my face with yours.

Pressing your heavy forelock to my mouth,
I long to feed you sugar, human horse.

In the Pavilion of Time and Infinity,
it seems for what feels like almost forever

that nobody again will ever die,
as if to stay alive is to keep talking.

Syllables spiraling out of its head,
my torso contorts into new poses.

For days at a time I repose on my clamshell.
Terrible flowers shoot out of my face.

One thing I'm sure of about the apocalypse
is that it looks really beautiful from far away.

Nothing

Every square is on fire
I ride by on my unicycle

Before I knew about plate tectonics
I didn't know about plate tectonics

The globe a seamless ball
Smoke billows handsomely

Over the country
I'm dancing in the cardboard box I am

As full of joy
As a pink window frame

I untwist my arms
Reassemble my face

Then stuff the news
Into my mouth until it's gone

No one will get me
To stop twirling my baton

I drape a flag over my head
Now I see nothing

Like the Union dead
But it's a flag of gauze

Does nothing mean zero
Or infinity

Is nothing a miracle
Or is everything

I drag a stick sword
Through the gravel making sound

The Nineteenth Century

The simultaneous presence of diverse orders

The leisure of critical thinking

An exchange of pleasantries with a multitude

Of characters

Ranging from the not interesting

To the deranged

And then we were running

Into the photogravure

As if from a thicket of whispering bugs

Or after a kite string

I recall a brief time

When I was twenty-three years old

We have covered the

Earth we have coveted

We patient

Bricklayers of war

Laying one on top of another

We bayoneted one another

While the dogs bayed

Until the last sound

Yet I remember Father's musics

A landscape of faces

The ruins were never whole

Still I recall a brief time

I wore an orange chiffon dress

And everybody turned

The Symptoms

Mold tinsels the berries. A fly swims the milk.
I reach for the wineglass and topple it over.
I turn on the faucet and watch the floor flood.
My nervousness blooms like a carrion flower.

The future arrives, filling me with velocity.
I am a ten-speed bike. I am a swarm of geese.
Now I have hundreds of wings.
Squawking, I overwhelm the fallow cornfield.

The last glacier melts as I'm draping my mouth
over somebody's fist. I will dance this slow night
on my elbows and knees. On the way to the end,
I drive up to a wedding and marry a stranger.

We circle, seven times, a holy fire.
We build a child, then build another child.
Passing for miracles in the right light,
screaming, they spin around the picnic spread.

The Empire of Light

The baby pulls my wrist into his mouth.
The baby wants to eat my face.
So does the dog, the one that I don't have,
who lazes at the razor-edge
of vision, whose curved shadow, when I'm still
flat on my back, opening up
like a gift the new morning, clouds over me.
The sister asks me to apologize for 1985
to '93. I screen all calls
from the persistent bank. The baker calls.
The baker wants her pie back.
Even the fan, worrying
the air from its perch on the ceiling,
sucks breath from my lung.
The future wants its diaper changed. I stroll it
past the drooping wisteria to the Family Dollar,
where I contemplate our next move.
In the suburban zoo, we gawk at cages.
We are surrounded
by musical notes of bright weather.
The panda turns its back on us
like an unhappy god.
I take the baby home. He'll live forever,
I'm almost sure. He laughs like fire laughs,

inexorable heat, blue flame unraveling.
I have barely begun the day,
I think towards evening.
The baby presses at my collarbone.
You know what makes us happy?
The whole world.
We're swaying to a prelude by Ravel.
We're waving good-bye
to the empire of light. Our destiny
is red, purple, and black.

Annunciation

The words I put in him he troubles with
and over, shifting in reverse the syntax of,
as though a poet troubling the line
with malaprop, but not a poet yet. He's three.
He's lived less time than most
of the anxieties I've nursed for him.
Please don't roll over on the other boy,
I whisper from the ball pit's burbling edge.
Three years after he opened into the fluorescent
annunciative light of the extraction room
his eyes, I case the boiling pit's perimeter
for his lit smile and fail
to understand one thing he feels,
this human foal, vortex of appetite, machine
of noise, child who won't blow
the softest sound into the pennywhistle,
this charming man who can't quite purse his lips
to activate the bubble wand, tiny muscles refusing
to hoist the necessary sails. The future promises
countless encounters with useless specialists
waving in his face wands, while tonight
my son waddles out three hours after being
put down, the muslin penguin
pajamas sagging slack at the hip,

to murmur to himself amid the assembled
living room wreckage of miniature trains,
with trancelike clarity, his eyelids half-glued,
this is my whole life, this is my whole life,
and my world too.

The World

out of blue distances out of closed rooms

out of the pavement and out of the mist

out of the hologram buildings

out of the bright machines and clatter

through the electric landscape we believe in

we wander here we collect ourselves

out of the architecture into the air

likewise in autumn likewise in spring

time pauses long enough for us to tune

the tiny radios inside our chests

we turn them up so we can hear each other

as people blow toward us like flurries of light

to tell us the names of the people they love

there are so many flowers

and all of them have names

we move ourselves around them almost dancing

into the stillness and into the wind

breath catching long enough for you to clutch

a stranger's hand

as people drift past us like clouds from a dream

we had once about the sky

Walkup

What awaits is another cluster of stairs.
If the child alternates his feet

he earns a hot cocoa and gets a gold star
stuck to his pullover. The fear

the child refuses to go far
without stumbling takes over the father,

eyes darting websites
across his black cell.

What awaits is another cluster of stairs,
the carpeted landing in between

an invitation for the child to stretch
his compact, hypotonic body

into a barricade, knocking his shoes
against the newel post and balustrade,

stirring his lips into an insurrection,
requesting to be raised into the air.

What awaits is another cluster of stairs.
What awaits is another flight of despair.

Once lifted, the child's body thaws
into crimped velvet. Like a heavy kite,

he flops and sputters, for a flash disrupting
the stairwell's windless atmosphere.

Each door unlocks distinct
discordant music

of enigmatic neighbors
muffling plans.

Each body spends a lifetime
softening

into the brick constraints surrounding it.
The bodies acquiesce to one another.

The child's hand spreads over his father's face.
What awaits is a final cluster.

Flag Day

The flags flew in the wind and I saluted.
We'd just moved out, my family, the lot of us,
from one country into another. I failed
to understand the consequence.

The flags clapped like the wind. I spent each yellow
bus ride attempting to count toward infinity.
My fellow children told me I was weird
and couldn't speak their language skillfully

enough for freeze tag. I replied *you're welcome,*
meaning *please.* Dear freckle-dotted, bowl-haired
adversaries who chased me merrily in tartan vests
around the shrubbery, chanting *USSR*

go home! in dissonant harmony, where did you
move, the lot of you? Each Flag Day, single file,
we strutted through the playground with French horns
and out-of-tune clarinets, some holding poles

aslant, like knights with spears, others saluting.
Nostalgia is a pathological sickness. Photographed,
I am as quiet as an apple approaching the mouth.
In the Pavilion of Din, my skull stays a silence.

The customs agent palmed the wedding ring
my mother had neglected to declare, unfastened
one gold Leo from a chain around her throat,
and called it contraband. My mother clasped

the thin residual chain, transporting it
over meridians in her breast pocket. Flags
danced drunkenly across the darkling field,
unspooled their languid torsos listlessly

into the limpid sky of possibility. I spent
every quarter I palmed from my mother
on yellow eggs in the store's prize machine.
One had a plastic ring inside. I handed it

to my impassive mother as she steered
a cart overloaded with staples: detergent,
Snapple. One heavy flag, unflappable,
ginormous, bore down its shadow over her, then me,

a consequence, a language, an infinity.

Exit Visa

Do you remember what life
was like in the Soviet Union?
They cracked open the potatoes
with their teeth. They cracked
each other's mouths agape beneath

the frosted sun, made furtive love with every
balalaika and guitar until the niveous
godless night vanished inside them,
red necktie tight against the thyroid gland
and trachea. O Pioneers! The pretty tractors plugged

away at the beige sandbox: *collectivization
will harvest a brighter tomorrow!* My future
mother first contracted into labor
as she watched sea turtles unschooled in Marx
swim placidly about their slowpoke business

replacing walls with an expanse of water
inside the nature documentary inside
the concrete cinema that kept her
away from hypothermic boulevards.
The nurses kept her in the ward one month.

The fault was mine: I rearranged her organs
with my enormous head. My comrades cracked
their teeth on frosted bottles, cackling
like birches at the opening of spring
through their new hollows. Life

was like everywhere, basically—do you
remember it, despite the lack of will,
scanning blurred eyes beneath the puffed ushankas,
the gray cortege of stairwells, and no,
you couldn't walk away from it, couldn't

rearrange your personal pattern of breathing
or write this poem. And yet, enough like everywhere:
the fluted shadows posturing along the trottoir,
one body rushing listlessly until the bus
eased to the corner and the doors swung.

My furtive mother has lost interest in dwelling
on the long subject of her hurried youth. She worries
the lost past will reach with its glass hook
around her neck and drag,
catch her back up in it.

The Anxious Journey

Before I boarded,
I gorged myself on banana and pineapple,
Folded and unfolded my softest gloves,
Ran a hard comb through the sweat of my hair,
Kissed my mother on the forehead,
Kissed my son on the nose,
Kissed my wife on the neck,
Held myself in my arms,
Kissed the conductor on the mouth,
Thinking that a difference could be made,
And then I boarded the strange train
And the reassuring moan of the locomotive
Made me think of the Canada geese
I pelted with bread, the warm fact of them,
Made me for a moment forget the journey
I spent my life readying for, though I still,
As the train thundered off,
As my fingers rapped gently on the darkening window
Of my final thought,
Saw the whole map fan out before me: inexorable, flat.

The Household

In a fenced-in Colonial, I tended my family.
On a damp Murphy bed, I pretended my family.

In a shotgun shack, in the radioactive valley,
we swayed to "Ain't No Mountain High Enough," my family.

Amid the stalagmites the bridge left behind
as it caved: a red Celica's spoiler, one-half of a family.

Why the divorced ornithologist wept:
even the titmouse and grouse had a family.

In my dad's favorite poem, the old Pict begs the Scots
to murder his son—his tribe's secrets must die with his family.

Happy Days. Family Ties. The Partridge Family. Growing Pains. Full House.
    All in the Family.
Family Feud. Married… with Children. Just the Ten of Us. Bonanza.
    Different Strokes. The Addams Family.

A family misplaces its son in a mall.
He might still be there, looking for you, Family.

Before you tie your hiking boots and strap that rucksack on, plant kisses, Stranger, on the foreheads of your family.

His body denting the fresh snowbank of campus,
the student thinks of algorithms, his roommate's argyle socks, the speed at
    which the trees are spinning past him, the snow, his cheek on it, a
    dance his feet once made, a mirror flying by, but not his family.

My father Lazaruses me two years after our brawl
so we could funeral his mother as a family.

If you must wander, Stranger, into your despair,
pour moonshine down your throat, make for the nearest train, thrash like a
    luna moth against a window screen, and, for your children's sake, unlearn
    your family.

On the cutting room floor, I tended my family.
In my life's motion picture, I pretended my family.

The People's Temple, the Moonies mass-marrying thousands, Charles Manson
and Family, The Children of God, also known as the Family of Love, or the
    Family.

Alone with moonlit brush, two girls trek the barbed wire
spanning a continent for weeks to recover their family.

For many years, I pretended my family.
After they died, I tended my family.

And you, my Dad, having forsaken me
a second time, resurrect me again, Sir: I'm family.

Wrong Funeral

The body opening the ground
was not the magic
trick I walked over the graves
to see performed,
was not the body I had prepped
myself, when tightening
a tie around my jugular
and jacketing my frame,
for mourning. I was not prepared
for this deceased. The body
hiding its breath in the wood box
for all I knew had been already
sawn in half, or disappeared
into a bird of handkerchiefs,
was not the beautiful
I came to bury, and when the relative
whose shoulder tried to hold
the wrong corporeal box
aloft in air, tripped from the weight
and landed on one knee,
as if proposing to an unrequited
love, an outtake in the gag
reel of a British comedy,
I could not keep my self's

composure, laughing louder
than I would at someone
pulling a rubber heart
out of their empty top hat.
The play was foul—each actor
missed their cue, had no idea
what to say. They stammered
through their lines like children,
like naughty children
telling lies for the first time,
knees tremoring the ground
we stood on. Heart out of control
like a malfunctioning
metronome, had I bought tickets
to this death, I'd want
my money back, a signed
retraction from the God
directing it. As if proposing
to an unrequited God,
I didn't want to be there,
but I stayed. Through every phoneme
of the clergy's hocus pocus,
I stood my ground, feeling the cords
inside my neck push back

against the tie restraining them.
Every dead body is a stranger
inside its magic box, each vanishing
a sleight of light. Trapdoors
landmine the topsoil
of the hollow grounds
we find, an accident, ourselves
saying good-bye to one another in.
I pull my rubber heart
out of my chest, a sleight
of hand throwing it down
into the hole with all the others,
then watch the earth stitch back
its seamless self,
until the hole, too, vanishes.

The Several Words I Have

You will never understand, try as you might,
a person other than yourself, controlling
an altogether different set of limbs. She was removing
her galoshes in the wet, insipid light. He was setting
the table for one, creasing the calm, paper napkin.
The world has lost its winters. We glisten in the sun,
each one of us a shiny obstacle to someone.
Is it the end of empathy? Of history? Who at this point,
navigating their browser through acres of weather,
has anything requiring being said? Why share
a knowledge no one wishes for? And is a poem just
a crack in time? Or is a poem time itself, continuing?
I may have mistaken motion for action
and action for proof, romping each night around
the phosphorescent dance floor, once a pretty dress
in a pretty hat, once a rumpled frog
under the awnings and parapets. My very appearance
at court caused astonishment. Now I recline
in my corner, delicate and mute, sheathing myself
in a leatherbound chair, shushing the migraine.
For whom did I mistake me, a president of some sort?
For who am I, a whistle in the exhaust?
It is all, nevertheless. I fail to tire of it.
I let go of the several words I have.

Little Soul, Restless and Charming

Animula vagula blandula
—Emperor Hadrian, on his deathbed

Python wrapped tight
around the soul inside
     the brain beneath
     the skull beneath
the skin shielding
the soul from the ultraviolet
     sunlight cast over the violent
     shadows of hills,
it has turned out
you are the greater emperor,
     guest and companion
     of our shambling body,
and we, who are about
to steer our dinghy
     into the open sea,
     salute you. As the nosebleeds
from which we have suffered
continue to intensify, we begin
     to despair of this our life,
     who were well known
for our aquiline features, who used to
ride, all at once, the gray ponies.

Now, when we aren't
drowning in a dream,
we pace through a room
without color, savage and bare.
No one will give us poison
or a sword, or smother us
with the indifferent
weight of their hands.
Who can imagine
a landscape without us.
We climbed Mount Etna
to witness one sunrise.
All we had wanted was
a pair of wings.
Little is left of the shell-
shocked factory:
dust on the floor, an over-
used machine.
A word is just
as thing as a bronze door.
The artist is only as good
as the art.
How cavalierly the unbolted
door swings open.

The Uncertainty of the Poet

Pressed in spring wool, wrapped in layers of white linen,
we have made camp in the imagined city,
enjoying its carousel and the occasional ice cream,

exchanging a passel of phrases with its other ghosts,
every word in the throat both a chasm and a choice
while time gets lost between the hulking alcoves

and molting birds. We zigzag each square
of this tilted city on pins
we have tangled our sounds in,

the sky a mystery we wander under
in figure-eights, in such infinities
of pattern we've lost track.

Thus, we arrange ourselves amid the statuary,
deciding to recuse ourselves from dying.
Have we succeeded yet?

If we had wings, would we fly everywhere,
riding the current of daylight?
A child rolls her hula hoop into the clock tower's shadow,

a child we made to understand ourselves,

a shadow herself in a sunshine of shadows.

We rush to board the train as it whips past.

Ordeal

The creatures throwing
bran muffin at me
from the back seat
of the Volkswagen SUV

stopped talking to themselves
and now take turns
becoming dinosaurs,
their happiest

of games. They are a torture
I talked myself into,
and as I ferry them, my favorites,
I notice with my tongue

that I have managed,
in my sleep, to lose
the sliver of one side
of a premolar:

a portioning out,
a judgment, from the German
urteil, that which the gods
dole out, one arduous deal.

Most end up lucky
never to have been
marched barefoot,
like Cunigunde of Luxembourg,

over red-hot ploughshares,
nor forced to swallow feathers
in dry bread,
nor made to carry

through a hissing crowd
the planks of wood
their fate will nail them to,
nor waterboarded.

Most of us are lucky,
yet when we smile, we draw
attention to the contours of the skull
beneath uneasy skin,

to the confusion
polluting the eyes,
startled like burghers
in a painting by James Ensor,

whose work makes clear
what scared him
in the tranquil afternoon:
the dignified

deteriorating faces smiling
into him as he traversed
a bridge or saw
a mirror. And the skeleton inside.

Myself I prefer to retreat
into the jellyfish dream factory
of my open eyes, as we traverse
the span allotted, each hillside

pedicured and tilled, a burst
of starlings hurtling
themselves in trapezoids
at the clay sky above us:

the brontosaurus, the triceratops,
and me, who loves them,
if love is the right term
for what the stand of hollow trees

feels toward its greening
canopy, for how night rain
scatters itself
over the eager topsoil,

for the extent to which I'm able
to luxuriate in light, inhaling
steam, though I suspect
I am succumbing,

gradually, to an identity
deficiency, an overpowering
lack of sense,
as I continue serving

(until it's time to ascertain
if the accused will sink
in innocence, or, obstinately, float)
what's left of my life sentence

with all of you beneath this wire
and bird, amid the tangled
shadows, root systems,
a congeries of slate rooftops.

The Idea of Order

I stand to my chin in the cyan sea.
Salt burns my nose when I look down.
Nothing is near that belongs to me,
and nobody for miles around
when my back faces the crowded shore.
The solitary understands
one's placement apropos the birds.
I am a cloud, or a silver machine.
Because I was raised by people, I became
bonded to people. I skipped
over the crabgrass with the other girls.
I laughed when they wanted. I ate what they handed.
Mastered the wind harp and Acrobat Pro.
Mastered Instagram and the sousaphone.
Much like a person, I have steeled myself
to like a person other than myself.
Still, secretly, I am, as you, a frightened god.
Birds skirl their warnings through the brisk, raw sky,
but I am become deaf, the destroyer of words,
submerged to my crown in the cyan sea,
chopping the spume with my many arms.

NOTES

"Skull of a Unicorn" is inspired by a gold unicorn skull overlooking the Grand Canal in Venice that Damien Hirst displayed as part of his 2017 exhibition *Treasures from the Wreck of the Unbelievable*.

"The Courtship" references the epic 1988 ninety-day walk on the Great Wall of China by the performance artists Marina Abramović and Ulay; their meeting halfway was intended initially to result in a wedding but instead resulted in a breakup, after which they did not speak to one another for twenty-two years. "It is always the others who die" was written on a piece of paper Marcel Duchamp carried in his pocket in the last years of his life; it is the epitaph on his grave. "There is no solution because there is no problem" is also a quote by Duchamp.

"The Double Dream of Spring," "The Anxious Journey," and "The Uncertainty of the Poet" were all written in conversation with eponymous paintings by Giorgio de Chirico.

"Clouds" references Andy Warhol's *Diamond Dust Shoes* series.

"East Liverpool, Ohio" refers to the city on the Ohio River that was once considered the pottery capital of the United States, but is now more known for its massive toxic waste incinerator and the heavy metal pollutants such as manganese and cadmium that it spews into the atmosphere. "I still exist," "I have decided not to commit suicide, don't worry," and "I have decided not to commit suicide, worry" are examples of text that appeared on postcards sent by the Japanese conceptual artist On Kawara (1932-2014).

"Garden of Earthly Delights" is loosely inspired by Hieronymus Bosch's eponymous painting. "The Pavilion of Time and Infinity" referred to in the poem borrows its name from an exhibition space at the 2017 Venice Biennale.

"Nothing" references Pope.L's iterative performance "Eating *The Wall Street Journal* (Flag Version)."

"The Empire of Light" is loosely inspired by René Magritte's eponymous painting.

"The Household" references the 19th-century Robert Louis Stevenson ballad "Heather Ale: A Galloway Legend" and the 2002 movie *Rabbit-Proof Fence*.

"The Several Words I Have" owes the idea of the poem as "a crack in time" to Valzhyna Mort, who articulated this concept during a Q&A session after a reading sponsored by Bennington College.

"Little Soul, Restless and Charming" takes its title from a translation of the first line of the poem "Animula, Vagula, Blandula," by the Roman Emperor Hadrian, addressed to the writer's soul and dictated on his deathbed. According to the Roman historian Cassius Dio, Hadrian "now began to be sick; for he had been subject even before this to a flow of blood from the nostrils, and at this time it became distinctly more copious. He therefore despaired of his life." The phrases "guest and companion of our... body" and "room without color, savage and bare" are translations of lines from the original poem. Additionally, Hadrian undertook the first recorded hike in history, to the top of Mount Etna.

"Ordeal" invokes St. Cunigunde of Luxembourg (c. 975-1040), Holy Roman Empress and wife of Emperor St. Henry II, who, to prove to him that she never committed adultery, voluntarily walked over red-hot ploughshares without her feet getting bruised. James Ensor (1860-1949) was a Belgian painter and printmaker associated with grotesque and morbid imagery.

"The Idea of Order" misquotes Vishnu in the *Bhagavad Gita* saying to Prince

Arjuna as he takes on his multi-armed form, "Now I am become Death, the destroyer of worlds," the quote Manhattan Project physicist Robert Oppenheimer, considered the father of the atomic bomb, uses to express his reaction to witnessing the bomb's first detonation in New Mexico in 1945.

ACKNOWLEDGMENTS

Thank you to the editors of the following publications, in which these poems first appeared:

The Academy of American Poets Poem-a-Day, *American Poetry Review*, *Bat City Review*, *The Believer*, *The Book of Scented Things: 100 Contemporary Poems About Perfume*, *Boston Review*, *The Brooklyn Rail*, *Colorado Review*, *Columbia Journal*, *The Common*, *Conduit*, *Connotation Press: An Online Artifact*, *Copper Nickel*, *Denver Quarterly*, *Harvard Review*, *The Hopkins Review*, *H.O.W. Journal*, *The Iowa Review*, *The Laurel Review*, *Ninth Letter*, *Pleiades*, *Ploughshares*, *POETRY*, *Poetry International*, Poetry Society of America, *Washington Square*, and *Waxwing*.

Some of the poems subsequently appeared in *American Odysseys: Writings by New Americans*, *The Brooklyn Poets Anthology*, *In the Company of Russell Atkins: A Celebration of Friends on His 90th Birthday*, *The Unamuno Author Series Festival Anthology*, and *In the Shape of a Human Body I Am Visiting the Earth: Poems from Far and Wide*.

The writing of this book was assisted by grants and fellowships from the Civitella Ranieri Foundation, the Headlands Center for the Arts, the Hermitage Artist Retreat, the Cuyahoga County Community Partnership for Arts and Culture, and the Ohio Arts Council, as well as by professional development grants from Bennington College.

Thank you to Four Way Books, and especially to Martha Rhodes and Ryan Murphy.

I will always be grateful for the generous insights of Rick Barot, Erica Bernheim, Jericho Brown, James Allen Hall, Katy Lederer, Cate Marvin, Sandra Simonds, and Phillip B. Williams, who donated their time to reading this manuscript as it took shape. And I am indebted to Monica Ferrell for her wisdom and love.

ABOUT THE AUTHOR

Michael Dumanis was born in the former Soviet Union and lived there until his parents were granted political asylum in the United States. He holds a BA from Johns Hopkins, an MFA from the University of Iowa Writers' Workshop, and a PhD from the University of Houston. The author of *My Soviet Union*, winner of the Juniper Prize for Poetry, and the co-editor of the anthology *Legitimate Dangers: American Poets of the New Century*, he is the recipient of the Lyric Poetry Award from the Poetry Society of America. He lives in Vermont, where he teaches at Bennington College and serves as editor of *Bennington Review*.

PUBLICATION OF THIS BOOK WAS MADE POSSIBLE BY GRANTS AND DONATIONS.
WE ARE ALSO GRATEFUL TO THOSE INDIVIDUALS WHO PARTICIPATED IN
OUR BUILD A BOOK PROGRAM. THEY ARE:

Anonymous (14), Robert Abrams, Michael Ansara, Kathy Aponick,
Michael Anna de Armas, Jean Ball, Sally Ball, Clayre Benzadón, Adrian Blevins,
Laurel Blossom, Adam Bohannon, Betsy Bonner, Patricia Bottomley,
Lee Briccetti, Joel Brouwer, Susan Buttenwieser, Anthony Cappo, Paul and
Brandy Carlson, Dan Clarke, Mark Conway, Elinor Cramer, Kwame Dawes,
John Del Peschio, Brian Komei Dempster, Patrick Donnelly, Lynn Emanuel,
Blas Falconer, Jennifer Franklin, John Gallaher, Reginald Gibbons,
Rebecca Kaiser Gibson, Dorothy Tapper Goldman, Julia Guez, Naomi Guttman
and Jonathan Mead, Forrest Hamer, Luke Hankins, Yona Harvey, KT Herr,
Karen Hildebrand, Carlie Hoffman, Glenna Horton, Thomas and
Autumn Howard, Catherine Hoyser, Elizabeth Jackson, Linda Susan Jackson,
Jessica Jacobs and Nickole Brown, Lee Jenkins, Elizabeth Kanell, Nancy Kassell,
Maeve Kinkead, Victoria Korth, Brett Lauer and Gretchen Scott, Howard Levy,
Owen Lewis and Susan Ennis, Margaree Little, Sara London and Dean Albarelli,
Tariq Luthun, Myra Malkin, Louise Mathias, Victoria McCoy, Lupe Mendez,
Michael and Nancy Murphy, Kimberly Nunes, Susan Okie and Walter Weiss,
Cathy McArthur Palermo, Veronica Patterson, Jill Pearlman, Marcia and
Chris Pelletiere, Sam Perkins, Susan Peters and Morgan Driscoll, Maya Pindyck,
Megan Pinto, Kevin Prufer, Martha Rhodes and Jean Brunel, Paula Rhodes,
Louise Riemer, Peter and Jill Schireson, Rob Schlegel, Yoana Setzer,
Soraya Shalforoosh, Mary Slechta, Diane Souvaine, Barbara Spark,
Catherine Stearns, Jacob Strautmann, Yerra Sugarman, Arthur Sze and
Carol Moldaw, Marjorie and Lew Tesser, Dorothy Thomas, Rosalynde Vas Dias,
Rushi Vyas, Martha Webster and Robert Fuentes, Abby Wender and
Rohan Weerasinghe, Rachel Weintraub and Allston James, and Monica Youn.